The Kids Guide to FORTUNE TELLING

written by **Louise Dickson**

illustrated by **Pat Cupples**

SCHOLASTIC INC.
New York Toronto London Auckland Sydney
Mexico City New Delhi Hong Kong

**To my lucky guy and my lovely girls,
with love. — LD**

Acknowledgments

The Kids Guide to Fortune-telling was based on an idea by Valerie Wyatt, my editor and new friend, and I would like to thank her for taking a chance on me. I would also like to thank Jane Tallim for introducing me, in her own delightful way, to Tarot card reading. Jane looks for a silver lining in every card she turns up. She taught me that fortune-telling could be good, clean, frivolous fun.

I want to thank my lovely daughters, Sarah and Tess Hunter, for getting swept away finding their lucky numbers, writing invisible fortunes and dropping pennies in dishes of soapy water.

Finally, I would like to thank my husband Iain Hunter for listening and laughing.

Edited by Valerie Wyatt

Designed by Marie Bartholomew

Cover photography by Ray Boudreau

Voyage through the future

When you wish upon a star or make a wish before blowing out the candles on your birthday cake, you're doing what people have done for thousands of years — hoping that something good will happen in the future.

Everyone is curious about the future. We want to know what will happen to us next week, next month, next year.

What does the future hold for you? Do you dream of traveling to distant lands or climbing mountains or even exploring new galaxies? Will you pirouette across a stage or somersault through the air on your way to an Olympic gold medal? Will your dreams come true?

The Kids Guide to Fortune-telling will show you old and new ways to predict the future, tell fortunes and amaze your friends. A pair of dice, a magic potion or invisible ink could hold the key to what might be, in a place where dreams come true.

Of course, no one can really tell you what road your life will follow. But if you want to make a little magic and have a lot of fun, read on. You'll have a good time — that's our prediction.

Were you born lucky?

You were born with a lucky number … but what is it?
No need for a crystal ball. Just grab a pencil and some paper.

1. Write down the month, day and year you were born, using all numbers. (Check "Months of the year" to find out the number of the month you were born.)

2. Add up all the numbers. For example, if you were born on November 10, 1988, you would calculate your lucky number like this:

$$1+1+1+0+1+9+8+8=29$$

month   day   year

3. You will end up with a two-digit number (29). Add the first digit to the second digit. Repeat until you get a number from 1 to 9.

$$2 + 9 = 11$$

$$1 + 1 = 2$$

Your lucky number would be

4. Check "What's in a number?" to see what your lucky number reveals about you.

6

Months of the year

January	1
February	2
March	3
April	4
May	5
June	6
July	7
August	8
September	9
October	10
November	11
December	12

What's in a number?

Some people say you can tell a lot about a person by her lucky number. What does your lucky number say about you?

Lucky number 1

People look up to you because you've got great ideas. But don't always insist on getting your own way.

Lucky number 2

You are fair and helpful. Make sure you also stand up for yourself.

Lucky number 3

Life is a roller coaster, and you love the ride. Don't forget to take along a little common sense.

Lucky number 4

You're good at organizing stuff. Remember to let loose sometimes and have a little fun.

Lucky number 5

You're an explorer and curious about the world. But don't get distracted — do what you say you're going to do.

Lucky number 6

You're a loyal friend, but sometimes you're too modest. Believe in yourself and take some risks.

Lucky number 7

You're smart and thoughtful. Remember that there's more to life than thinking. Take time to play.

Lucky number 8

You're reliable and steady and plan to make a lot of money. Don't forget to have some fun along the way.

Lucky number 9

You're charming and funny. You have lots of friends. But not everything in life will be so easy. Effort is its own reward.

What's in a name?

Is luck your middle name? Here's how to find out.

1. Write out your full name.

2. Using the "Letter numbers" chart, write the matching number under each letter.

Letter numbers

A	B	C	D	E	F	G	H	I
1	2	2	4	5	8	3	8	1

J	K	L	M	N	O	P	Q	R
1	2	3	4	5	7	8	1	2

S	T	U	V	W	X	Y	Z
3	4	6	6	6	6	1	7

3. Add up the numbers. For example, if your name was VICTORIA BAIRD, you would calculate your lucky name-number like this:

V I C T O R I A
6 + 1 + 2 + 4 + 7 + 2 + 1 + 1

B A I R D
2 + 1 + 1 + 2 + 4

= 34

4. You will end up with a two-digit number (34). Add the first digit to the second digit. Repeat until you get a number from 1 to 9.

3 + 4 = 7

Victoria's lucky name-number is

5. Check "The name game" to see what your name-number tells about you.

The name game
Just for fun, see what your name spells out for you.

Name-number 1

You have bad taste in swimsuits.

Name-number 2

You actually like broccoli.

Name-number 3

You're hard to get up in the morning.

Name-number 4

You like to disco dance.

Name-number 5

You have a lot of bad hair days.

Name-number 6

You watch too much TV.

Name-number 7

You drive your parents crazy.

Name-number 8

You like pets more than people.

Name-number 9

You have hidden talents.

Windfall winnings

Will you be rich or poor? Flip some coins and see where your luck lies.

1. Toss ten coins into the air. For every coin that lands on tails, count one. Count nothing for heads.

2. Add up the ones and check "Count yourself lucky" to see how fortunate you'll be with money.

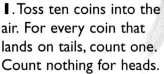

Count yourself lucky

If your coins add up to

Here's what you should do

0	Don't flip out. Try again.
1	Keep an eye out for loose change. (You're going to need it.)
2	Get a paper route.
3	Ask for extra allowance.
4	Save your pennies. Don't raid the piggy bank yet.
5	Take a trip to the candy store.
6	Open your own bank account.
7	Cash a check from a doting relative.
8	Count your change carefully.
9	Give generously to others.
10	Get ready to strike it rich!

What will today be like?

You never know how a day is going to add up — or do you?
Find out by calculating your day-number.

1. Write down the month, day and year, using all numbers. (Check "Months of the year" on page 7.)

2. Add up all the numbers. For example, to find the day-number for September 12, 1998, you add:

$$9 + 1 + 2 + 1 + 9 + 9 + 8 = 39$$

3. You will end up with a two-digit number (39). Add the first digit to the second digit. Repeat until you get a number from 1 to 9.

$$3 + 9 = 12$$

$$1 + 2 = 3$$

The day-number for September 12, 1998, is 3.

4. To find out what's in store, check "Your daily forecast."

Your daily forecast

Day-number 1

Be bold.
Do something different.
Phone a new friend.
Read a new book.

Day-number 2

Work hard.
Do your homework or help around the house.
Today, work first and play later.

Day-number 3

Rest, relax and unwind.
Give your muscles and your brain a holiday.

Day-number 4

Get organized.
Clean your sock drawer.
Find your homework – then do it!

Day-number 5

Head outside and enjoy nature.
Pack a lunch.
A long walk is just what you need.

Day-number 6

Plan a family outing — go for a hike or a picnic.

Day-number 7

Have some fun and laugh a lot.
Invite a friend over.
Plan a party!

Day-number 8

Learn a new skill.
Grab a skateboard, a tennis racket or a basketball.
Practice makes perfect.

Day-number 9

Be creative.
Do some sewing.
Make some jewelry.
Work on a tree fort.
Paint a picture.

Weather dreaming

Have you ever had a dream about the weather?
Some people believe weather dreams can reveal what your day will be like.

If you dream of　　　**It means**

a rainbow　　　　　You'll have happiness, joy and good fortune.

rain　　　　　Your luck will change. A dry spell is over.

a storm　　　　　Uh-oh! You may fight with a friend.

thunderclouds　　　　There's trouble ahead.

fluffy white clouds　　Better keep your feet on the ground.
　　　　　　　　　Your head's in the clouds.

lightning　　　　　You'll be struck with inspiration.
　　　　　　　　A new idea will suddenly hit you.

fog　　　　　You're confused. Don't make any big decisions.

On a roll

Can the future be foretold by a roll of the dice?

Shake three dice and throw them onto a table. Add up the numbers shown on the dice and check "A fortune in numbers" to see what your future holds.

Dots of fun

If a roll of the dice has you seeing spots, try fortune-telling with a set of dominoes.

1. Spread a full set of dominoes facedown on a table.

2. Mix the dominoes thoroughly and then choose one.

3. Add up the dots on both parts of the domino you chose and check "A fortune in numbers" to see what's in store for you.

A fortune in numbers

1   You'll follow a new and exciting road.

2   The waiting is finally over. Your patience will be rewarded.

3   Make room for someone new in your life.

4   Get packing — a journey is not far-off.

5   A surprise is in store. Hope you like it.

6   Be careful. Trouble could be just around the corner.

7   Unlucky today, lucky tomorrow. Your luck will change soon.

8   An act of kindness will bring you a reward.

9   Don't tie up the phone. Someone is trying to get in touch with you.

10   Is it a check? News from a pal? Watch the mail!

11   Don't count your chickens before they're hatched.

12   Someone you like has special feelings for you, too.

13   Don't step on anyone's toes. You could end up fighting with a friend.

14   Stop looking — a treasure you lost will be found.

15   You will have a narrow, hair-raising escape.

16   Good times are on the way.

17   If it feels good, do it. Learn to trust your instincts.

18   Your wish will be granted.

Four square fortunes

Pets? Kids? Job? City? Do you want to know about your future life?

1. Draw a large square on a piece of paper.

2. Write four questions, one along each side of the square.

3. Under each question, write down four possible answers. They can be serious or silly.

4. Pick a number between 1 and 10. Or use your lucky number. Let's say your lucky number is 5.

5. Put your pencil on any answer and start counting. For example, if you start counting at Ferret, it would be number 1. Tarantula is number 2. Keep counting until you land on Miami, which is number 5. Cross out Miami.

6. Move to the next answer and start counting again. In this example, you would start counting to 5 again from The North Pole. Keep counting and crossing out answers until there is only one answer left for each question.

7. Now put all the answers together: You will be an actor who lives in Timbuktu with one child and a tarantula.

The Moon

Timbuktu

The North Pole

Miami

Where will I live?

Soccer player

Archaeologist

Deep-sea diver

Actor

Iguana

Horse

Tarantula

Ferret

What pet will I have?

What will I be?

How many children will I have?

1

2

4

8

Wheel of fortune

Put a new spin on fortune-telling and make your own wheel of fortune.

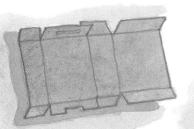

You will need

a pen or pencil

an empty cereal box

scissors

a paper fastener

1. Cut the cereal box apart and lay it flat on a table.

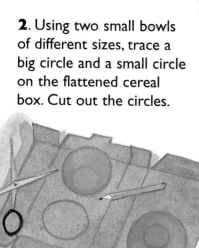

2. Using two small bowls of different sizes, trace a big circle and a small circle on the flattened cereal box. Cut out the circles.

3. On the blank side of the small circle, draw an arrow pointing to one edge.

4. Around the edge of the big circle write Happy, Hectic, Fun, Exciting, $$$, Rewarding.

5. Center the small circle on top of the big circle and secure it loosely with a paper fastener. You should be able to spin the top circle easily.

6. Ask, "What will my day (or week or birthday or life) be like?" and give the small circle a spin. The word closest to where the arrow points is your answer.

Folding fortunes

Fold up this fortune-teller and amaze your friends with your ability to see into their futures.

You will need

a 20 cm x 20 cm
(8 in. x 8 in.)
piece of paper

a pencil

a ruler

colored pencils

1. To find the center of the piece of paper, draw diagonal lines from corner to corner. Fold all four corners in to touch at the center.

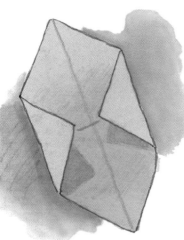

2. Turn the paper over. Fold these four corners into the center. When you've finished, you'll see eight triangles on the side of the paper facing up. If you flip it over, you'll see four squares.

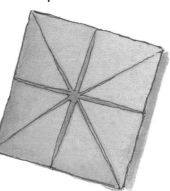

3. Fold the paper in half so that the triangles are inside. Now fold it in half again. Crease the folds.

4. Unfold the paper so that it looks like it did in Step 2. Lift the triangles and write eight fortunes, such as Good luck, Bad luck, A Disagreement, on the back of the triangles.

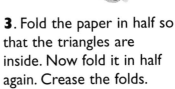

GOOD LUCK!   BAD LUCK!

5. Write the numbers from one to eight on the front of the eight triangles.

6. Turn the paper over. On each square draw and color a creepy crawly — a scorpion, a spider, a caterpillar, a slug and so on.

7. Slip your thumbs and index fingers under the squares. Press the points together as shown.

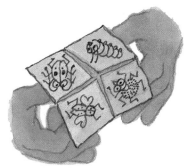

8. Open your fingers. You should see four triangles with numbers on them. Open your fingers the other way. Four different triangles appear.

9. To tell a fortune, ask a friend to choose a creepy crawly. If she chooses a spider, for example, spell the name out loud S-P-I-D-E-R. Open the fortune-teller in opposite ways as you say each letter.

10. Now ask your friend to choose a number. If she chooses five, open the fortune-teller five times. Ask your friend to choose one more number. She can turn over that triangle and read what the future will bring her.

Wishing on a star

Yes! No! Maybe! Probably! Do you have a question you're burning to ask?
Wishing on a star may give you the answer.

You will need

a pencil

paper

scissors

1. Cut a five-pointed star from a piece of paper.

2. In pencil, lightly write Yes on one point, No on the second point, Maybe on the third point and Probably on the fourth point. On the fifth point, write "Your dreams will come true."

3. Put the star under your pillow, with the writing facedown. When you go to bed, ask the question you want answered, then tuck up one point of the star. Don't peek. Every night, for the next three nights, fold up one more point. On the fifth night, the unfolded corner will give you the answer to your question.

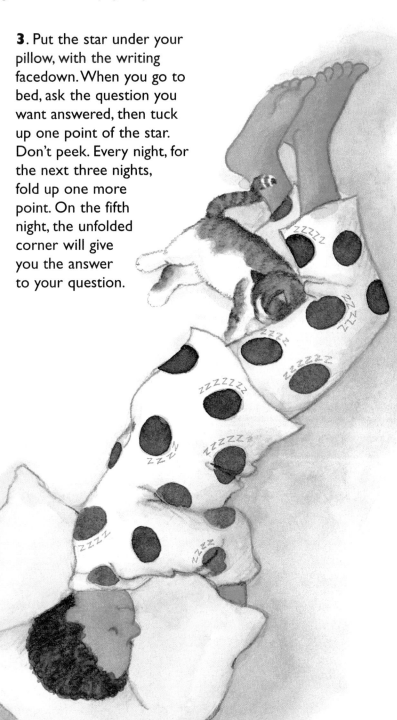

The secret of the seven slips

Combine invisible writing with fortune-telling
and surprise seven friends.

You will need

a lemon, cut in half

a small bowl

a ball-point pen or
toothpick

seven small slips of paper

a box

a candle

2. Let the slips dry thoroughly. This might take up to 30 minutes. Place the slips of paper in the box and mix them up.

3. Have seven friends each choose a fortune.

4. Ask an adult to help you warm each slip of paper over a burning candle. Be careful not to burn the paper or yourself. The fortunes will appear as the heat from the candle darkens the lemon juice.

1. Squeeze the lemon juice into the bowl. Dip a ball-point pen or toothpick into the lemon juice. Use the toothpick to write one short fortune on each of the seven slips of paper.

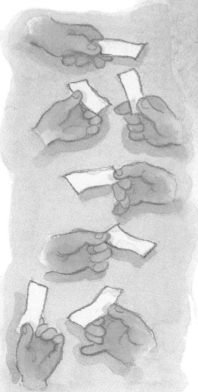

Peel me a prediction

Long ago, when people had an important question to ask, they would use an apple peel to find their answer. You can try it, too.

Peel an apple carefully so that you end up with one long, unbroken peel. Ask your question, then throw the peel over your shoulder.
If it falls in the shape of a U or an O, the answer is No. Anything else spells Yes.

Twist of fate

Hold an apple in one hand and twist the stem with the other as you recite the letters of the alphabet. The letter you are saying as the stem breaks off is the initial of your special friend-to-be.

Gone to seed

What lies ahead? Good luck? Bad luck? Uncertainty? To find out, cut an apple in half and count the number of seeds in the core. An even number of seeds means good fortune is headed your way. Find an odd number and you may be in for a disappointment. If one of the seeds is cut in half, your future will be unsettled.

The apple of your eye

Stand in front of a mirror and press a fresh apple seed to your forehead so that it sticks. Quickly start to recite the alphabet. The letter you are saying when the seed falls off is the initial of a new friend you are about to meet.

A sticky situation

When you can't make up your mind between two friends or two parties or two sports, let an apple make the decision for you. Take two apple seeds and name them for your choices. Stand in front of a mirror and stick both seeds to your forehead. Don't forget which is which. The one that sticks longest will tell you which option you should choose.

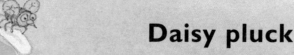

Daisy pluck

Have you ever plucked the petals off a daisy one by one while reciting "Loves me; loves me not"? The answer is whatever you are saying as you pluck the last petal. Flowers can be used to predict other things in life, too. Pick a flower, pluck some petals and choose a rhyme.

Going to a birthday party?

She'll call me.
She won't.
I get invited.
I don't.

How will I do on my next test at school?

Fail.
Pass.
Top of the class!

What will the weather be like on my birthday?

Rain or snow?
Sunshine's glow?

A new best friend?

We'll be pals,
Friends forever.
Now we're fighting.
Friendship?
Never!

Blowing in the wind

A dandelion can tell you if your wish will come true. Find a dandelion that has gone to seed. Close your eyes, make a wish and try to blow the seeds off the dandelion.

If all the seeds fly off, your wish will come true.

If some seeds remain, blow again. The number of blows it takes to remove the seeds is the number of months that will pass before your wish comes true.

If none of the seeds blows off, you're out of luck. Blow harder next time.

Ask a dandelion a Yes or No question. If the seeds float up, the answer is Yes. If they float to the ground, the answer is No.

Cheep predictions

Have you heard the saying, "A bird in the hand is worth two in the bush"? Ancient fortune-tellers thought otherwise. They believed that two blackbirds in a bush was an omen of great fortune. Here are some other flying fortune-tellers.

If you see	It means
a bluebird	happiness
a crow	unhappiness
a dove	peace
an eagle	power
a seagull	travel
a hummingbird	love, marriage, new life
a lark	good health
an owl	wisdom
a robin	a happy home
a stork	children
a wren	good luck

Love and marriage

Can love be found in the letters of your name? A stroke of a pen may reveal the answer. In this game, match your name with the name of someone you like and see what your chances of marriage are.

1. Write out your first and last name.

2. Now write out your special friend's first and last name.

3. Cross out each letter that is the same in your first name and his last name.

4. Cross out each letter that is the same in your last name and his first name.

5. As you cross out the remaining letters in your name, say,

"Love, Hate, Friendship, Marriage, Love, Hate ..."

What are you saying as you cross out the last letter? It is supposed to show you how you feel about the other person.

6. Cross out the remaining letters in your friend's name, saying,

"Love, Hate, Friendship, Marriage, Love, Hate ..."

How does your friend feel about you?

How many children
will you have?

Skipping stones and counting seeds may help you count your future blessings.

Skip a stone across a pond and count the number of skips. You will have one child for each skip.

Eat an apple and count the number of seeds in the core. That's how many children you will have.

Blow dandelion seeds into the air and catch as many as you can. The number you catch will tell you how many children you'll have.

Who will marry first?

At your next sleepover, take some thread and tie your big toe to your friend's big toe. In the morning, when the thread is broken, check to see whose toe has the longest thread. She will be the first to marry.

Words on the wave

Can a floating fortune-teller predict the future? Get on board and give it a try.

You will need

paper

scissors

a pen

a bowl

4. Ask a Yes or No question as you pour water on the pieces of paper. The slip of paper that rises to the surface first will give you your answer. If the blank slip rises first, it means fortune doesn't have an answer for you yet.

1. Cut out three small slips of paper.

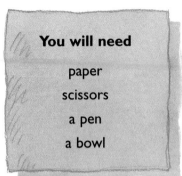

2. Write Yes on one slip, No on the second slip and leave the third slip blank.

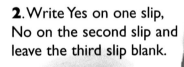

3. Place the three slips in a bowl.

The secret of the bubbles

How many friends will I have? How many weeks will I stay at camp? How many years before I own my own horse? Here's a fortune-teller to answer those "how-many" or "how-long" questions.

1. Fill a bowl with water and add a squirt of dish soap.

2. Ask your question, then quickly throw a pebble or coin into the water.

3. Count the bubbles that rise to the surface. The answer to your question is the number of bubbles you count.

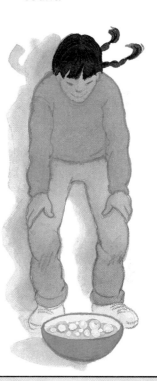

Dough buoy

Do you have a question that can only be answered by Yes or No? Ask your question and then toss a crust of bread onto the water. If the bread sinks, the answer is Yes. If the bread floats or washes up on the shore, the answer is No.

Potion predictor

Your friends will boil over with curiosity when you mix this fortune-telling potion. The answers to their questions will foam and bubble before their eyes.

You will need

125 mL (1/2 c.) water

125 mL (1/2 c.) water mixed with 15 mL (1 tbsp.) baking soda

125 mL (1/2 c.) water mixed with 15 mL (1 tbsp.) vinegar

a bowl

1. Ask your friend to think up a question about the future that can be answered by Yes or No.

2. Tell him to choose two of the three liquids and pour them into the bowl as he asks the question.

If the potion bubbles, the answer to the question is Yes.

If there is no reaction, the answer is No.

Body omens

Can your body tell you what's going to happen in the future? Some people think annoying little itches, coughs or hiccups are your body's way of predicting events. What do you think?

If this happens   **It means**

Your ears are burning  Someone will get in touch with you.

Your right ear is itchy  You'll hear some good news.

Your left hand is itchy  You're going to lose money.

Your right hand is itchy  You're going to find money.

Your feet are itchy  You're going on a trip.

You sneeze  You need a tissue.

Telling tea leaves

You don't need to be a gypsy to read tea leaves. Here are some tips.

You will need

a teapot

15 mL (1 tbsp.) loose tea leaves or a tea bag

a white teacup

1. Put the loose tea leaves into the teapot or rip open a tea bag and empty it into the teapot. Ask an adult to pour in enough boiling water to make one cup of tea. Let the tea steep for a few minutes, then pour the brew into the teacup.

2. Carefully pour off the liquid until only the tea leaves are left in the cup.

3. Shake the leaves until they coat the cup.

4. Look for shapes in the leaves. What do the shapes suggest to you? Let your imagination wander or check "Shaping the future."

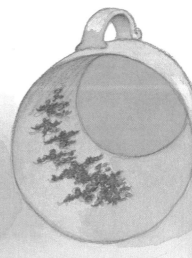

If the leaves are close to the brim of the cup, something special will happen soon.

If the leaves are at the bottom of the cup, you'll have to wait for your fortune.

The handle of the teacup symbolizes your home. If you see "birds" (tea leaves) "flying" toward the handle, expect good news.

An unclouded future

Flop down on the grass and watch the clouds billowing by. Can you see faces or animals moving across the sky? Take another look and check "Shaping the future." Maybe there's a message in the sky for you today.

Shaping the future

If you see		It means
a fish		You'll be swimming in money.
a fiddle		You'll be invited to a dance.
a hippo		Time to tighten your belt.
a snake		Someone will cause trouble for you.
mountain peaks		You're climbing toward success.
an anchor		You're going on a voyage.
a hand		You'll make a new friend.
a parrot		Mischief is brewing.
flies		You'll be irritated, annoyed or worried.
a clock		Act now or you may run out of time.
a feather		Take yourself more seriously.

The hand of destiny

Your destiny is in your own hands — at least fortune-tellers think so. Many people believe the lines on your hand show what will happen during your life.

You will need

washable paint

a paintbrush

a piece of paper

a magnifying glass (if you have one)

1. Brush a light coat of paint onto the palm of one hand and press it onto the paper to make a handprint.

2. Use the diagram on this page to find your heart line, your head line, your life line and your fate line.

Your **life line** is thought to tell how long you will live and how healthy you will be. A long, unbroken life line means a long and healthy life. A broken life line means you may face health challenges in your life.

Your **fate line** tells about your successes and failures in life. A strong, unbroken line means you'll get what you want and have many successes. A broken or thready line means setbacks, but if the line continues, you'll get what you want through hard work.

Your **head line** tells how your mind works. A straight line across your palm means you think things through. A slight curve means you are creative and artistic. If your head line runs downward, you think for yourself and are imaginative.

HEART

HEAD

LIFE

FATE

Your **heart line** tells how loving and friend you are. If other line cross your heart line, your love life will be storm If your heart line is unbroken, your friendship and love will always be returned.

Palm close-up

Use a magnifying glass to look for other shapes
in your palm print.

A **star** means a windfall. You will come into money.

Straight lines on the middle joint of your little finger mean
you'll never have to worry about money. (This person isn't so lucky.)

A **square** on your life line means you'll be protected and safe.

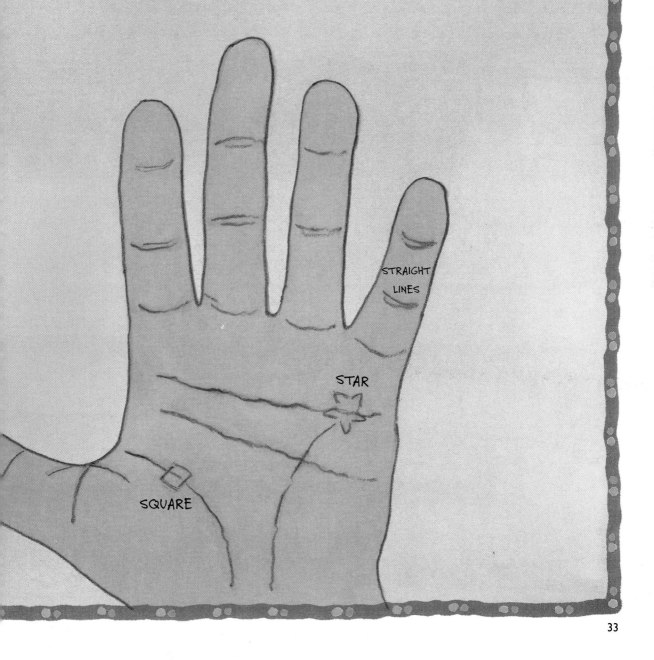

STRAIGHT
LINES

STAR

SQUARE

A swing of the pendulum

Fortune-tellers believe the movement of a swinging object can help you predict the future.

You will need

a button

a string about
30 cm (1 ft.) long

1. Tie the button on to the string.

2. Sit at a table. Resting one elbow on the table, hold the free end of the string between your thumb and index finger. The button will hang down, forming a pendulum.

3. Keep the pendulum still and ask a Yes or No question. Wait. Eventually the pendulum will begin to swing.

• If it swings in a circle, the answer to your question is Yes.

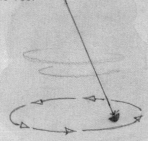

• If it swings back and forth, the answer is No.

If your pendulum seems to be giving you crazy answers, ask it a question you already know the answer to. Ask, "Am I a boy?" and see which way the pendulum swings. Let this be your guide for figuring out future answers.

Ringing in the future

Tie a long thread to a ring. Lower the ring-on-a-string into an empty glass and hold it steady.

Ask a Yes or No question. When the string starts to move, count how many times the ring knocks against the glass.

• One knock and the answer to your question is Yes.

• Two or more knocks and the answer is No.

Dream omens

Many people believe dreams contain symbols that foretell the future. Write down your dreams every day in a dream journal. In a month or so, look back and see if any dreams have come true.

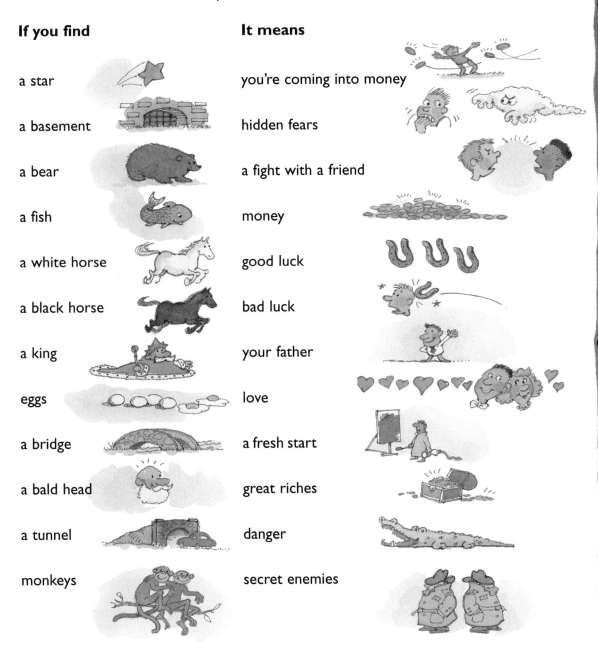

If you find	It means
a star	you're coming into money
a basement	hidden fears
a bear	a fight with a friend
a fish	money
a white horse	good luck
a black horse	bad luck
a king	your father
eggs	love
a bridge	a fresh start
a bald head	great riches
a tunnel	danger
monkeys	secret enemies

Make your own fortune cookies

You don't need a crystal ball to predict that people will love these light, sugary cookies. Before you make the cookies, write fortunes on tiny strips of paper. This recipe will make about 24 cookies, so you'll need the same number of fortunes. Now you're ready to get cooking.

You will need

250 mL (1 c.) cake flour

125 mL (1/2 c.) sugar

45 mL (3 tbsp.) cornstarch

a pinch of salt

3 egg whites

125 mL (1/2 c.) vegetable oil

45 mL (3 tbsp.) water

2.5 mL (1/2 tsp.) lemon extract

1. Preheat the oven to 150° C (300° F) and lightly oil a cookie sheet.

2. Sift the flour, sugar, cornstarch and salt into a bowl.

3. In another bowl, mix together the egg whites and oil.

4. Add the egg mixture to the dry ingredients and stir until smooth.

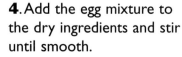

5. Add the water and lemon extract. Stir again.

6. Drop six spoonfuls of batter onto the cookie sheet. The batter should spread out into a circle about 7 cm (3 in.) across.

7. Bake the cookies for about 10 minutes. While they are baking, prepare a little egg-white glue by beating an egg white until it is foamy.

8. When the cookies turn a light golden brown, ask an adult to take them out of the oven. Work quickly — as the cookies cool, they begin to crack. Flip the cookies over on the warm cookie sheet. Place a fortune in the middle of a cookie. Spread a little egg white glue around the edges. Fold the cookie gently in half and hold it closed until the two sides stick together. Repeat until all the cookies contain fortunes.

The shape of things to come

Long ago, people who wanted to predict the future sometimes poured oil onto water and tried to decipher the omens revealed in the shapes it formed. To try it yourself, slowly pour a spoonful of cooking oil into a bowl of water. The oil will rise and float on the water's surface. Watch carefully.

If the oil	It means
forms a star	You'll be very lucky.
breaks into two parts	You'll fight with a friend.
breaks into many small globs	Money is coming your way.
spreads thinly over the water's surface	Troubles are ahead.
forms a ring	You'll be a success.
forms a crescent shape	Luck is on the way.

Lucky charms

It's a British custom to stir a coin or a ring into Christmas pudding. Finding a coin is supposed to mean good fortune. Finding a ring means you'll be the first to marry. You can make a cake and fill it with lucky charms for your friends and family.

1. Wrap some charms in waxed paper. See below for a list of charms you might want to use.

2. Make your favorite cake batter.

3. Stir the charms into the batter and bake.

If you find	**It means**
a ring	You'll marry young.
a thimble	You'll marry late.
a bell	Your life will be full of sweet music.
a letter	You'll write a dozen books.
a wishbone	You'll be a success.
a nut	You'll have good luck.
money	You'll be wealthy.
a button	You'll have to mend your ways.
a key	Doors will always open for you.

Are you fortune-nut?

If you and your friends are nuts about fortune-telling, you can make Fortune Nuts together. Write fortunes on tiny slips of paper. You'll need one fortune for each nut. When you've done that, get cracking.

You will need

a nutcracker

walnuts in their shells

a nutpick or small fork

glue

colored ribbon

3. Insert a fortune into one half, then glue the two halves back together.

4. Wrap a ribbon around your Fortune Nut and give it to a friend.

1. Carefully crack open a walnut. The two halves shouldn't be broken. (This may take some practice.)

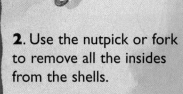

2. Use the nutpick or fork to remove all the insides from the shells.